Poems for the Queen of Heaven

Catharine West

BookLeaf
Publishing

India | USA | UK

Presentation by *BookLeaf Publishing*

Web: www.bookleafpub.com

E-mail: info@bookleafpub.com

ISBN: 9789360949440

First edition 2024

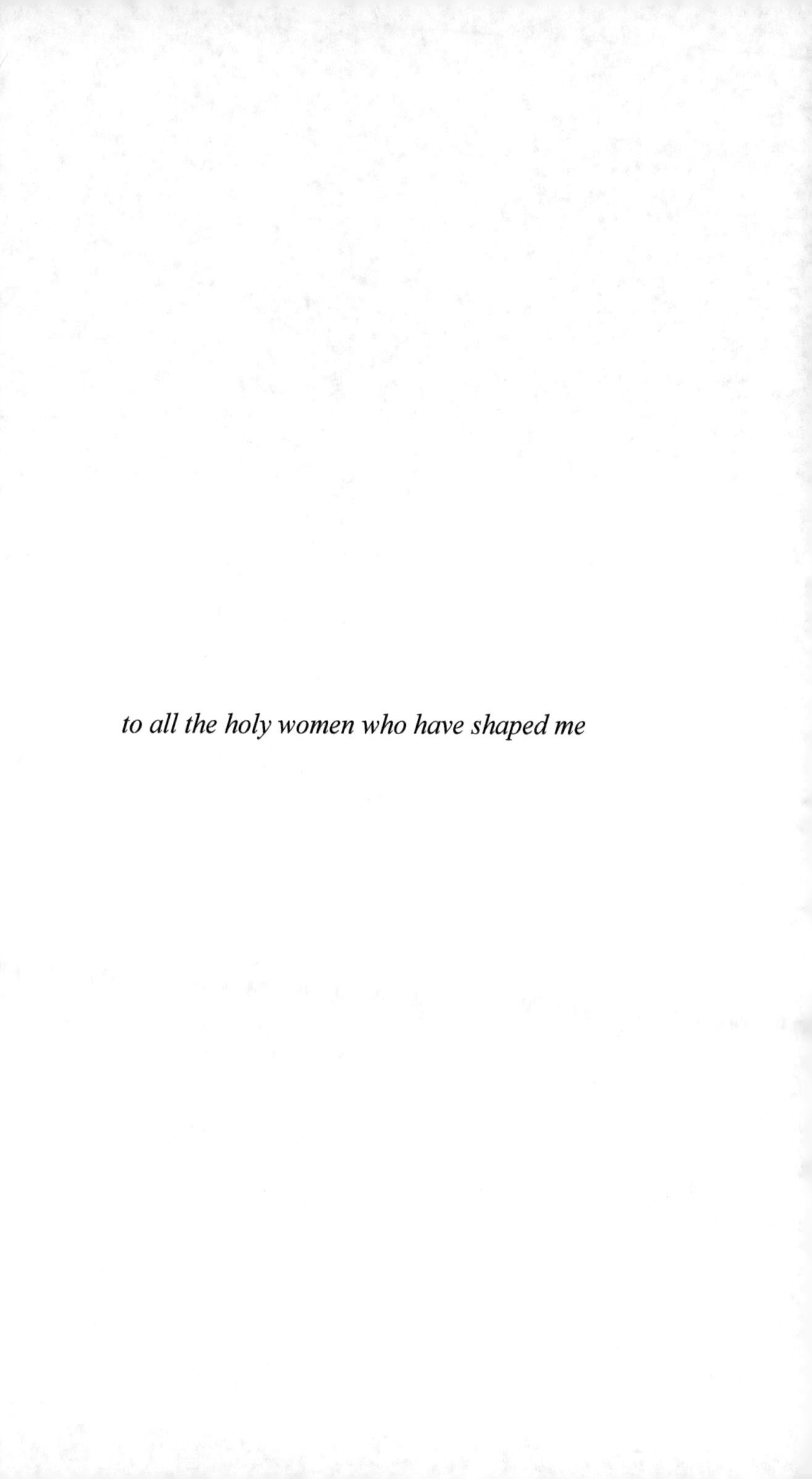

to all the holy women who have shaped me

Asphalt Grotto

You were no part of my faith.
I wasn't raised to see you
and was taught for those who did,
You were at best a misguided distraction
but more likely an idol.
I wasn't looking for another mother
and grimaced when a friend said
to look to you,
that you would suit me better
than the warmongering father
we refused to believe in
one moment longer.

She's not even a god, I thought then,
the mother—
a servile drudge, so weary and commonplace,
esteemed for being self-less.
It seemed still patriarchal to me.
I was not about to worship
the trap I avoided,
it makes us so small.
Her body just a vessel
her heart pierced with arrows
by the father and the mob
who demanded blood.

No, none of that.

I preferred other saints
pregnant with purpose,
The ones who disagreed with men
set them straight,
crossed entire seas in defiance,
built things, started shit,
did things they were free to do
precisely because they weren't
any body's mother.

But it's you who tends my garden now
roses sprawling all around you
in a grotto made of asphalt
chipped up from the driveway.
I built you a shelter here.

What lies they tell us
to diminish the power of women.
Only a God could give birth to a god.
You were worshiped before
he was ever even a story
in some small man's imagination
who wove a tale that made violence noble,
redemptive even, humans flawed
and women just mothers.
I don't believe in that god anymore.

Neither are we keeping
the old lie
that mothering is the deepest kind of love.
Too many of them prove that wrong.
Too many others love better
even without the labor of the womb.
But what does it mean
to adore Mary without
believing in the father or the son?
All over this house
I've made a shrines to you,
most beautiful creator of life.
Sacred heart shining,
feet on the warm earth,
beads in your hand,
a crown of stars in your hair.

I want my little girls to see
holy women,
to see and to be as divine
love as the force that brings
peonies up from the ground
and makes tomatoes burst on the vine,
in kisses from the dog who has our hearts
and in the songs of the birds we feed.
You stand here a power that
protects and affirms and adores
that shimmers
like the hum of the world.

Thrift Store Marys

You weren't blonde,
but you are here.
I take you home anyway.
Kentucky's not as Catholic
as it used to be,
as I need it to be
to complete this quest
to fill a too-high shelf
with thrift store marys.
My 'sky grotto'
my husband calls it,
and though you mean nothing to him,
I do,
so he lugs out the ladder happily
any time I bring a new mary
home.
We like you there
towering over us
encased behind glass
that was covered in a veil
of black film until a few months ago.
This old house continues to surprise us.
The longer I'm here
the more of you reside with us,
Our Lady of Bethel Academy.
Pray for us now in the era of our disbelief.

Miraculous Medals

You dangle from my ears today.
An older woman complimented them.
I saw recognition in her eyes
and tried to send it back with my thanks.
Your devotees are everywhere,
even running the cash register
at the discount store.
The glint in her eye said we are
possessing more secrets than we know
though the world says
we know nothing and are worth less.
These fake gold coins with your imprint
keep showing me how many see you
and how we love how abundant we are.

Talking at 2 am

She didn't stand up for the baby.
Left him with the mean grandmother
because her son told her to,
so she did.
And then called me
for sympathy.
I'm so mad
I can't sleep, Mary.
These mothers aren't mothers
and I cannot earn that name
no matter what I do
or how much love I give,
but I'd never obey that shit
and told her so.
She forgot she left us
with a screaming lunatic too,
left us by staying,
refusing to stand up to
the father
who beat her
and her son
and menaced us all.
That's an abused person's thinking, mom,
that you had to do what he said
and leave the baby alone.

It was a mistake to say,
but it's true.
She gasped, caved in.
Now I'm the bad one.
I alone have done
the unforgivable thing,
making real the consequence
of what she thinks
we all agreed
to pretend never happened.
Nobody stood up for us, Mary,
and nobody taught us about you.
Just a man on a cross
because his daddy's love
was violent too.

Iftar

The only church I've felt lately
has been with people whose
faith is not mine,
but God is there
in the radiant faces of young women
whose labor brings us together
feeds our bodies
nourishes our souls
I don't have to believe in anything,
just them.

Holy Virgin

When I was younger
a guy in the dorms
tried to rattle me
by saying "maiden" just meant
"young girl" and maybe
you weren't a virgin at all.
Not being Catholic,
this made no difference to me
whatsoever.
Your purity never mattered much,
though I've thought about
that conversation
a dozen times since.
I'd like you even better that way, I think,
your story then the spunk
of a knocked up teen
claiming divine intervention,
blaming the whole thing on God,
and then men took it and ran with it,
a scam you kept up for centuries.
And in the middle of their
violent theologizing
they write for you
a legacy of perfection.
It'd be so funny,

such a victory,
if they hadn't punished women
with the impossible model
of your sexless maternity.
Out here telling on themselves,
they admitted they defile things
by making the only holy woman
in the book
the one they didn't touch.

False God

The demiurge makes more sense.
A foolish god
who thought he was the only one,
embarrassing the adults in the room,
mad he failed to keep
his creation in the dark.
Children dream of their dolls
coming to life
and know better than this
jealous guardian demanding blood
that the fun of the fantasy
is when they no longer
rely upon the movement
of your hand.

The Word

The scribes' poison pens
have sickened us with filth
and called it god.
Violent mythmakers afraid of Eros
ruined even the parts worth keeping,
hellbent on hierarchy,
lashing us with the Word.
The price is as high as meaning.
We make sense of the world
out of the stories we know.

Wisdom holds the paradox.
The further from belief in God
the more devoted to you I become.
I unfasten the verses
and let the shape of my breasts show.
After all, what the fuck
is the book of Job?
I'm so proud now of my child self
who could not glean from it
any lesson worth learning,
who thought better of god
even then.
We are not mere playthings
callously handled by deities

in a cosmic feud,
one upping each other
like pedants in
some grad school seminar.

My search for you
undid my knots.
No dismembered concubines
further the plots
of my sacred texts.
No exchange rates for
raped daughters,
no lewd voyeurs or jealous gods
lurk in my gardens.
The peppers I grow here teach more
than those men will ever know.

Midnight

We stayed up late
expecting the snake,
hearing the music the third time
for him, the hundredth for me.
I've watched her sing and dance
all summer and fall,
a pied piper
leading us nowhere
but delighting the world's girls
as she builds an empire
of kindness and joy.
I think she might
know about you.

Marie Laveaux

Disbelief is a terrible loneliness
I vanquish with surrogates,
tender deities, causes,
projects, promotions,
things tacked on that take up time,
redirect my attention.
I'm just a biting puppy.
Just when it seems trained,
it remembers the taste of your palm,
the soft flesh and firm bone underneath.
Nothing tastes quite as good,
but I'll chew the chair leg instead
if I have to.
Zora gave me another mary
and this one has some teeth.
This one feeds me meat,
though she isn't meant for me.
She's the first I find
worthy of my offerings
and gives my hand
something to grasp.

Green Tara

Green Tara shares my name.
I find for myself a godself.
This goddess of compassion
refuses manhood when
it's presented on a platter
like John the Baptist's head.
No need, she says,
more enlightened than the givers
who perceive in her refusal
a sacrifice.
Maybe she'd evolved
beyond exteriors, sure,
but maybe she relished her form
or the soft curve of another.
No more divided bodyminds.
Men who cannot conceive
of a world where
they are not the center
no longer limit my stories.

Our Father

Redwing boots and a Stanley thermos
Vantage cigarette between his lips
One deep wrinkle
across the forehead.
Avid reader with a bit of college
Planned to teach history
and driver's ed.
Hopped on at the railroad
when babies were on the way.
Violent temper and a problem solver
loved and feared and respected at work.
Lawn expert who made his
liquor store runs to the neighboring town
so the church folks wouldn't see.
Backyard philosopher and a
kitchen table theologian
who outversed every preacher
we ever had.
He was a jack of all trades
who could fix anything,
but it wouldn't be pretty.

Dead twenty years now
and I wonder
What kind of man did he want to be?

Not the railroader he became.
He was a clean-cut mayor's son,
no, stepson,
and that mattered.
I worry he was not well loved
as a little boy.
His mother was cold at
strained holiday dinners.
He relinquished his first son
to his second of three wives.
What kind of dreams did he dream?

Why didn't they leave that shitty place?
What makes a rut seem like an abyss?
We made an idol out of him.
Now I've lost the tenderer memories
and see only the red fury on his face
as he beat my little brother
or his stern wild eyes
when he would direct us to our rooms
so he could fight our mother
in ways he knew we shouldn't see.
There was much more to him than that
and I have the good sense
to be grateful for
much of how he raised me,
but that's what sticks.
Just another sad little man
in the middle of nowhere

stomping around his shabby home
trying to feel like a king.

Trash

Today I'm lucky enough
to listen to a writer I love
share a poem he wrote
about being called 'trailer trash.'
We were never called that.
We had a house, after all.
'White trash' though once
overheard in the dormitory bathroom.
'Those sisters are really pretty,
but they're white trash.'

I don't hear stories like mine
in the hallowed halls of academia,
so I was really moved to hear
this writer tell a story
whose details I can taste.
No matter the slogans on the wall,
we definitely don't welcome all
in these temples of learning.
I am good enough now to no longer feel
the need to prove myself.
Most days I feel it's a scam.
I vacillate between these poles
thinking I've pulled off a magic trick
making a living out of books and ideas

or thinking myself a fool
of a middle-class pyramid scheme.
But then he saved a life today
sharing what he wrote.

In the Garden

Gold finches found the feeder today
and the pear trees are in full bloom.
I don't know if they're the good kind
or the bad kind
and frankly I don't care.
In my heart of hearts
I don't think we're gonna be here in five years.
Maybe just the birds in the trees.
We've done too much damage
to deserve to stay.
A vulture picks a carcass
on the side of my road home.
I hope they'll all be fine
left to their own ways once
the ocean drowns us all,
or the solar flares fuck up our computers
and we starve rather than coexist.
Maybe the invasive honeysuckle
will cover our bodies
and the red columbines will mark my grave,
flowers I'm re-introducing to my yard here
that our predecessors covered in asphalt.
They amputated tree limbs
to make room for their RV.
Men just like to use their tools

without thinking of the cost.
I've come around to that story
that used to annoy me,
good old Candide
with his wise instruction
to simply tend our gardens.
After all this time
and all this study,
it's all I know to do.
What better plans could one make
to ride out the end of the world?

Tomatoes in Fanjeaux

I had to go to France
to learn to like tomatoes.
For thirty years
I waved them off,
cold and wet
or worse, slippery, dripping—
there's no good word
for that interior
barely solid enough
to keep hold of the seeds.

I didn't want to eat them
that evening meal,
but our attentive hosts
worried at the space on my plate
since I don't eat meat.
They heaped them on
the empty spot
with a salty piece of fish
that I could not refuse.
I didn't know until right then
that American stores
sold only threadbare imposters.
Nothing had ever
tasted like this.

Now I dream of tomatoes.
They ripen perched atop a short list
with puppies and sea shells,
things that make me
believe there might still be a God for me,
one worth worshipping.
Cherry globes plucked from my vines,
taut yellow ones sliced thick,
eaten at the kitchen counter,
a pretty red one chopped up small
mixed with mayonnaise and saltines,
salt and pepper. Tomato cracker salad
with a coke. Old lady food.
I'll eat them any way.
Tomato summers mark my years
and make the littlest one
seem like my real daughter,
she loves them just as much.
What gifts, these fruits.

The Magnificat

You sing of a god we should fear
who lifts the low and honors you,
Theotokos,
she who gives birth to the one who is god.
I'd rather sing to you,
she who is more than a vessel,
she who becomes Creatrix
of the so-called savior of us all.
She who comforts the low of every land
who holds the wounded
like the infant in your icons.
Not a new eve but a
a fresh morning
a swaying daffodil in
the warmth of the sun.
A god herself whose power
manifests without
grotesque crucifixions.

Perennial

On Holy Saturday I planted
a rose bush next to you
from the multiflora shrub
that keeps returning
where she was first planted.
I moved her that first summer
to a spot that made more sense,
but some stubborn root remains
and sends up new vermilion
stems just to delight me.
It's just like that rose
from my favorite witch movie
that grows wild where they buried
the abusive man they killed.
No pruning back defeats it.

We won't be honoring tomorrow
the resurrection of a man-god
from violent death—
no more crosses for us here—
but I'll walk with my daughter
to the spot in the yard
where you keep poking up your head
and we'll debate how long
to let you grow before

I dig up again
your latest gift.
That befits a holiday.

Apparitions

My shitty grad school apartment walls
had poems taped up to the ceiling.
Snippets of others' words
that spoke truths to me.
I wish we had more of yours.
It seems you're a better listener
speaking with your presence,
showing up to say something
you don't need words to say.

Chiesas

I'm suspicious of big churches;
something's just too slick.
If that many people are
happy with the pastor,
he's not stepping on their toes.
I admit I love magnificent cathedrals
but I was more charmed
by the soft magic of tiny chapels
tucked in the streets of Siena.
They're scattered all over the city
like confetti.
You're on every guest list.
Everyone wants you at their party.
Like kids on the playground,
we always run back to our mother.

Mother of Sorrows

My mother is confused that her son, my brother,
conflates suffering and love.
Where could he have gotten such an idea?
From the God of Job and Abraham?
From our religion of the blood?
Or from her own relentless martyrdom
that tyrannizes us even now.
From family lessons that love forgives anything
someone might do.
Pretend you weren't up half the night
and cover up the bruises.
We thought ourselves one of
the nicest families in town,
but I wonder how much people knew.
The place is so small you couldn't hide
red eyes and tired children.
I wonder did her sister talk about
the times she tried to be a buffer.
Were we the reasons for Sunday whispers
and sideways glances?
If anyone offered rescue, my brother never
knew.
Folks shielded their eyes according to the rules
of midwestern middle-class manners,
We played this game with others.

One summer night neighbors screamed
and our parents did nothing.
They didn't call out to inquire
or call anyone to come see.
What makes a people so proud of themselves
for minding their own business
while children cower in corners
wondering if their mother
will make it through the fight,
while daddy weighs the cons of shooting himself
in the garage now that
the rage has boiled over?
She's asking a stupid question
on Good Friday of all days,
hours before they'll go to church together
to meditate on their contaminated souls
spared only by their tortured god's rebirth.

The Missing Madonna

What if I had grown up with you?
I knew your name only as a wild popstar
whose music my young mother danced to
when my father was away.
Would I have asked you to keep me safe at night
when the creaks and cracks made me think
someone was breaking in?
Would I have asked you to intervene
in the real dangers, which lived inside the
house?
Would you have soothed my tears and fears?
Would my understanding of good girl
have been narrower still?
It was the only protection I had.
Would I have cloistered myself and taken vows
to be with no man other than God?
Would that option have been a blessed relief?

I can see the ways it might go wrong,
but I think the balance would've come
out in my favor
had your icons been on my altars.
We're both owed an apology
that I was taught to see you
as no more than a holy door mat,

a paver for the star
of the gory sacrificial show.

Your immaculate heart
might've saved mine
from some of its breaking.

www.ingramcontent.com/pod-product-compliance
Lightning Source LLC
La Vergne TN
LVHW010835200726
843508LV00012B/2610